NSO MARRIAGE CUSTOM

METHOD OF WIFE ACQUISITION

LAWRENCE SHANG FONKA
AND
WILLIAM BANBOYE

Revised and Republished by Margaret Fonka Niba

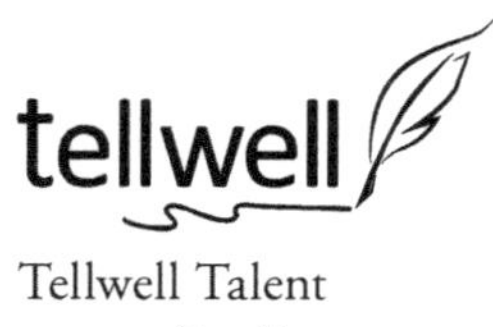

Tellwell Talent
www.tellwell.ca

ISBN
978-0-2288-3507-3 (Paperback)

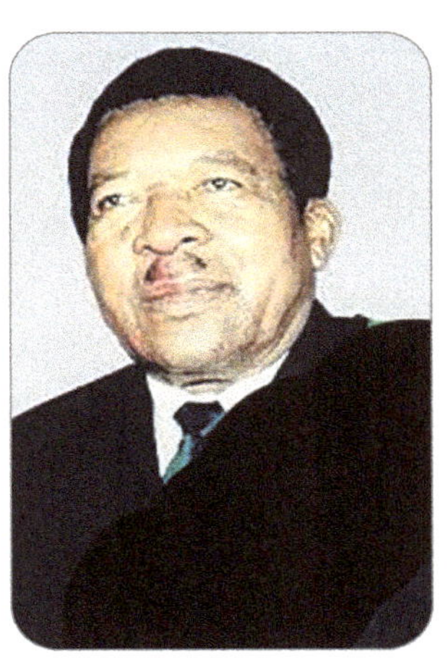

Honorable Fonka Shang Lawrence a professional teacher and Former president of the National Assembly of the Republic of Cameroon

Acknowledgements

Thanks to Erik Asongwe, artist who was patient enough to make same sketches over and over as described to capture the concepts portrayed to him to the best of his ability.

Greatest acknowledgement to his Royal Highness the Fon of Nso and the Nso Development Committee for encouraging me to reprint the book and for their efforts to safeguard and promote the rich Nso tradition.

Gratitude to Hon. Fonka Shang Lawrence, Mr. William Banboye, and Dr. Dan Lantum who did their utmost to preserve our rich tradition in the original book. Last and most importantly thanks to God Almighty for giving me the power and wisdom to immortalize out culture.

Forward

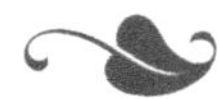

by Margaret Fonka Nba

It is about nearly thirty years since my dad died. During these years I toyed with the idea of reprinting and distributing my father's writings, "the Nso Marriage Custom and Methods of Acquiring Wives" co-authored by Mr. Banboye and "The Folk tales of Nso" with stories written by Mr. Vincent Jaff and William Kakiyi all of whom taught me in primary school and later some of them taught me in secondary school. These writings give me the opportunity to immortalize not only my father but also a group of men who relentlessly and passionately educated a lot of Cameroonians particularly children from Nso. Through these books these authors made sure that some aspects of the Nso tradition were not forgotten. Being a Nso daughter in the diaspora, I have noted with dismay, yet admiration the zeal of the Nso people to get in

Preface of the book

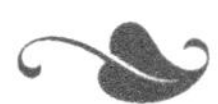

by Dr. Dan Lantum

*T*his Pamphlet is the expression of the long desire to preserve the Nso customs and tradition in a permanent record. We have for years since the coming of the white man suffered a gradual loss of our traditional wealth because we were preoccupied with acquiring their ways if we had to survive in the so-called modern world. This has reached a climax having to substitute one foreign European civilization for another. We look back and ask, "What had we before European tradition overtook us?" This pamphlet gives the answer regarding Nso traditional marriage which has now lost its place to the modernized mixture of cultural practices.

I am happy to note that the authors have left out purposely I believe this "modern" concoction which has evolved in the past decade and which will continue to evolve being highly influenced by the economic situation of Nso, its social advancement and its bombardment by foreign cultures. The work enjoys the fact of its publication by the Nso natives who appreciate the significance of customary marriage in the context of Nso customs and traditions. For want of better expression or more accurately for expression of a native idea absent in English culture in English, the authors have sometimes been forced to use lamnso to maintain the original ideas.

One does not necessarily need to agree with the details of the subject matter, this subject being capable of delicate controversy in parts, but one would not hesitate to say that this is Nso culture written by men of Nso personality.

I am sure this will satisfy the hunger already existing since in the absence of the Nso News Journal. I wish that everyone in Nso and even in the entire Cameroon would like to own a copy.

To Fonka and Banboye, I am grateful for their kind invitation to write this preface.

Dr. Dan Lantum, M, B.S (London)
Proprietor and Editor Nso News Journal.

Table of Contents

PART ONE

By L.S. Fonka

Nso Marriage Custom in General

Contrary to the traditional practice by several African tribes, the Nso people have no bride price. This is a peculiar feature that has stood the test of time against the practice by other Tikari tribes of Mezam. Other peculiarities in the Nso tradition as compared to the other tribes of the same origin include the fact that the first daughter of a woman is given in marriage by the maternal grandfather of the girl. Marriage gifts on behalf of the girl should not exceed those given on behalf of her mother.

In normal circumstances three houses receive marriage gifts. These are the immediate parents of the girl, the maternal grandfather (ta-yiy) and the maternal great grandfather (tayiy bam). Daughters born of unorthodox unions (kinchem) must get married in unorthodox way too. A father had the responsibility to initiate arrangements for his son to build his first house and to marry his first wife for him. Men are considered paupers if they cannot choose a wife for themselves.

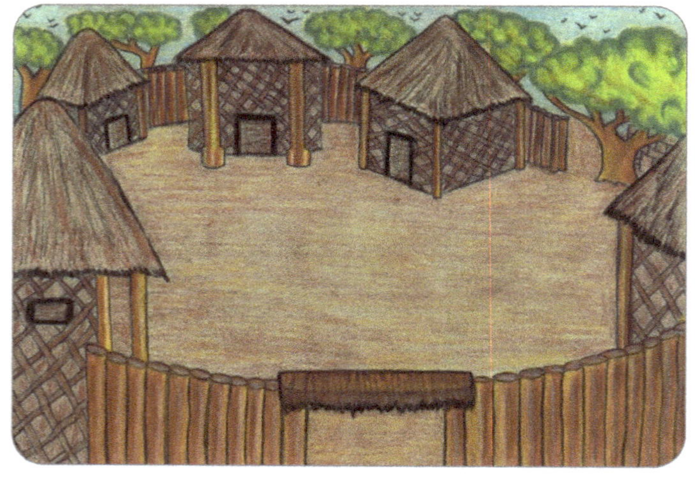

Old traditional compound built with bamboo,
mud and roofed with grass

Approaches to Marriage

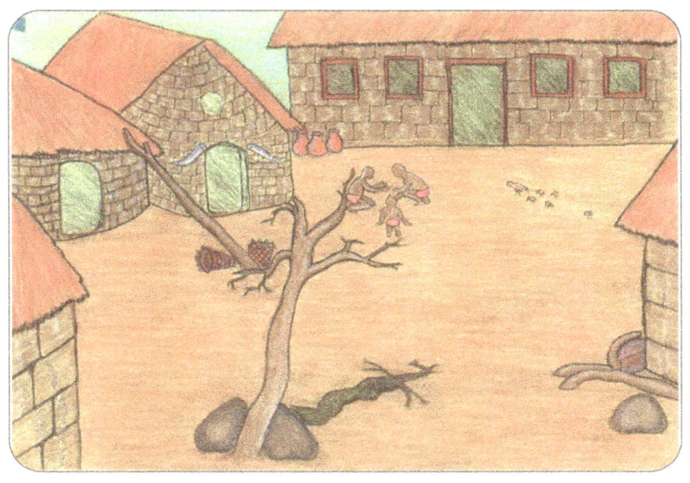

Current traditional compound built with sun dried mud blocks and roofed with corrugated iron sheets.

Customary Approaches to Marriage

Direct Approach

There are two approaches to marriage according to the Nso custom. The direct approach occurs when a man seeking a bride from a family goes to the girl's father carrying a calabash of palm wine (kitem ke melu) and a pod of kolanut not split open (ketam ke bih kefur la wa) as seen below.

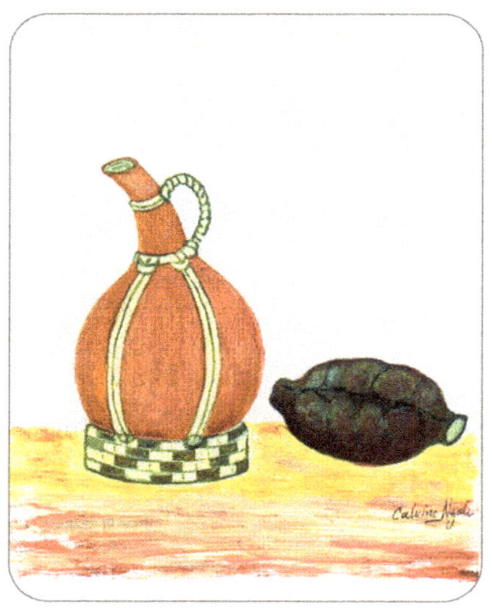

calabash of palm wine and pod of kola nuts.

Humbly, he begs for a dish of vegetables made from cocoyam leaves (mbar) or he simply states, "I am dying of hunger". If the girl's father and his family drink the wine and do not give money equivalent to the cost of the wine, it indicates that the man has been accepted as a son-in-law. If money is paid back less than or equivalent to the cost of the palm wine, it shows that the man needs to pay another visit with more wine. This action does not prevent humble, patient, and persevering men from paying another visit. Very often this refusal gesture is a test of the man's temperament which in a way determines the character of the man and his suitability to marry their daughter. Sometimes the girl's family shows admiration for the humility and perseverance of their future son-in-law by paying for the actual cost of the wine after drinking it. This gesture sometimes encourages the guy to pay another visit so that the girl's family can get more familiar with him. After he has been accepted, he goes back home and announces the good news to his family stating that he is officially a future son- in law (Sejuu). If the kola nut is returned as it was given, not split open, the man is rejected. If it is not returned at all, his request has been granted. If the father of the man goes to represent him, the girls' family will tell him to go and inform his son that he should continue the visit which his father has so aptly and kindly initiated.

Indirect Approach

The indirect method occurs when a young man, having spotted a compound where there are many girls develops a kind or generous and helpful attitude towards the people of that compound without expressing his intentions. Activities include inviting the head of the compound (Fai) for a cool refreshing drink in private, paying frequent visits to the compound during important occasions and helping to promote these occasions. He may offer gifts such as firewood, tobacco and other services to the compound had (Fai). The compound head recognizes understands and appreciates the man's activities as an indirect application for a wife. One day after one of these kind gestures, the compound head asks his most respected elder, "What can we best reward this good boy for his kindness". Sometimes it is the elder who approaches the compound head on the issue. The two men begin to investigate the would-be suitor to find out if he has any blood relationship with any family member in the compound. They also want to know if there exists an old grudge between the man's family and theirs.

Grudges include confiscation of the family's raffia bush, kola nut trees, or any property by the man's family. The two men try to find out if any man in the man's family ever committed adultery with one of the wives of their family. If thorough and honest investigations find that none of the above impediments exists, the young man's father or his father representative is invited to meet the boy's future father-in-law who now declares, "We have found your boy a good chap and we intend to give him food" The compound head and the elder of the girl's compound declare that there are no impediments and therefore the man will be given "food". The transaction at this stage is carried out over a drink of palm wine provided by the host. The guest returns home with good news.

Introduction of the Girl to her Suitor

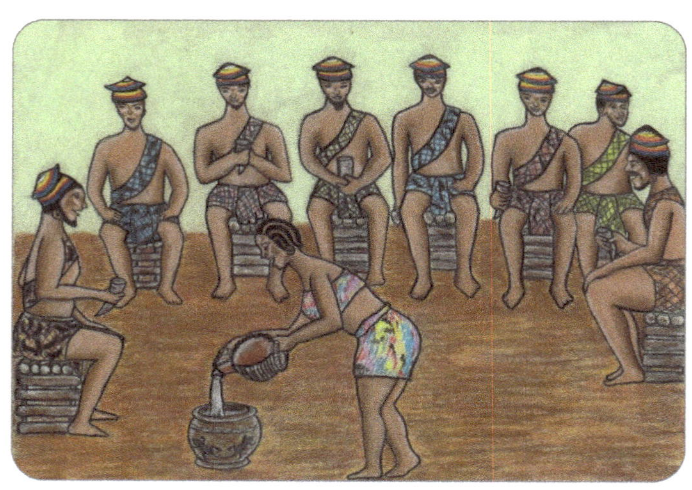

Pouring of wine into the wine pot

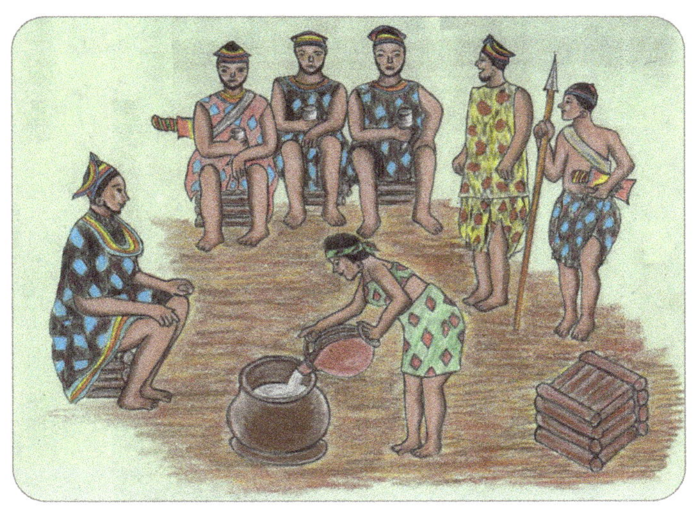

The compound head and elders of the girl's
family watching the girl pour wine

The visit that comes after a girl has been promised to a young man is usually grander than the previous ones. The boy and five of his relatives bring five calabashes of palm wine one of which is given to the elderly man of the compound (Tata wo mandze) in whose house the visitors usually call before they are taken to the compound head. The elderly woman of the compound leads a line of women to greet the guests. She steps in the house and asks, "Where shall I turn?" (m'to fe?). She is told to turn to her right. The remaining four calabashes of wine are taken to the compound head (Fai) who invites the elders as well as the girl who is the bride-to be to the assembly hall of the compound head (Shu Fai). The compound head orders two of the four calabashes of wine to be placed before his people. He asks the elderly woman of the compound to tell the girl that the young man sitting near the corner has brought this wine on her behalf and that she is expected to pour the wine in the family wine-pot for the elders of her family to drink. It is customary for the suitor to sit in an inconspicuous location. Very shyly she steals a look at her suitor, pours the wine into the pot amidst applause, serves the compound head and quickly rushes out. If she is very shy, she can make herself unavailable until the visitors leave. From his hidden location, her suitor catches a glimpse of his future bride as she pours and serves the wine. Usually he smiles. Part of the wine is sent to the women and the rest is given to the men. All are happy that their daughter has accepted a husband without pressure. Some girls are difficult at this stage particularly if they have personal objection to the visitors. Often, when some of these girls get curious, they spy on the visitors to appraise the suitors before this great moment arrives. In a polygamous set up, there are usually many girls of marriageable age at same time. The suitors are unable to determine who is being wooed until the girl concerned is invited to serve wine.

Visits after the Girl Has Been Introduced to the Suitor

Tradition demands that there be three visits every week after the introduction of the girl to her suitor. During the first visit, the suitor and family bring camwood (Bii) in a new raffia bag (kibam) and a carcass of a deer. Other gifts include vessels of a special type of corn beer (Nkang Kinyav) and a calabash of palm oil. The final gift prior to the marriage is salt. The amount of salt given depends on the ability of the giver. This salt is shared among the women of the girl's compound. A clever suitor before leaving the girl's compound, bribes an influential woman of that compound with the hope of motivating her to expedite the marriage arrangements.

After a week or two following the betrothal ceremony in the girl's village four women of the girl's family go to see their daughter's future home for the first time. This visit is called the "Kile-ei lav". The "Kile-ei lav" delegation also brings gifts such as maize (Ngwasang), millet (sang) and guinea-corn (sar) in small raffia bags. It is this delegation that sets the wedding date.

The suitor's family must give the delegation the impression that their daughter will have a happy home. This impression is given in the sumptuous entertainment given to these visitors and the amount of money put in the raffia bags. Cowries were used as a medium of exchange in ancient times. If these visitors are satisfied, they will announce the wedding date in secret before leaving. The guests call two elderly or responsible woman of the suitor's family and whisper to them that the bride should be expected in about three weeks. Should these visitors leave without announcing the date, it is a sign that they were not satisfied with their reception. The suitor's family reacts by sending a woman after the visitors carrying gifts like an empty raffia bag, a bar of salt (Kong-Shingwang) a calabash of palm oil pleading to the girl's family to set a wedding date. This request is done immediately. Another delegation of women is sent from the girl's compound to announce the wedding date (Ka' vijin). Reception this time is lavish to overwhelm the visitors who now give a three weeks' notice for the wedding to take place.

Wedding Preparations

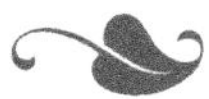

Both families prepare for the wedding ceremony. Preparations in the girl's family include fattening of the bride, and collection of marriage gifts (nko se vigin). These are special parcels brought along by the bride's family in the marriage procession to the groom's compound.

The fattening process of the bride (yo'gin) includes, resting at home, regular baths, and painting with camwood (Bii) twice a day and a special diet. The girl's immediate family, representatives from the maternal grandfather (tar-yiy) and the maternal great grandfather (tar-yiy bam) participate in the fattening process. In some cases, a rich or well-off suitor sends the cam wood (bii) to the girl's family. If the girl was popular in the area, her friends bring delicacies like honey, sugarcane, peanuts, and meat. This period lasts one week in the case of a commoner's daughter and two weeks in the case of a princess (wantoh) or a daughter of a lord (kibai). Custom allows the girl to visit her boy friends in the area during the fattening process (yo'gin). This special social activity (toni-nte) occurs in secret and at night. Only natural circumstances such as menses and distance prevent these visits.

The suitor's family prepares for the wedding by collecting lots of palm wine, food, chickens, and money (cowries in olden days). They also arrange extra accommodations like bamboo beds and rooms because they will be expecting a great number of guests at the nuptial celebration.

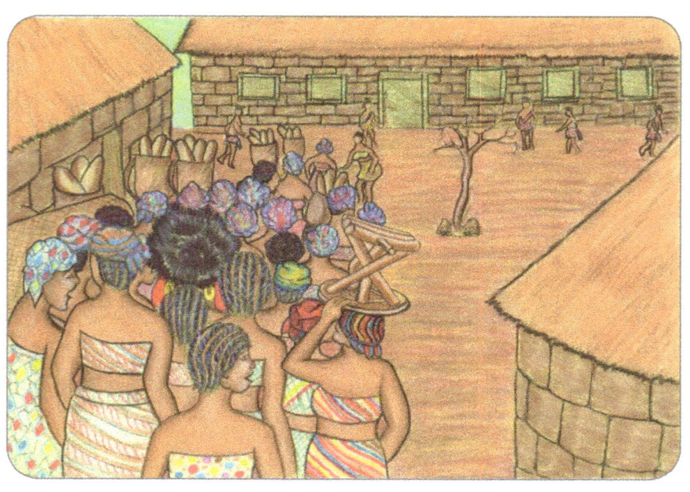

Bridal party arrives at the groom's compound

Arrival of the Bridal Procession to the Groom's compound

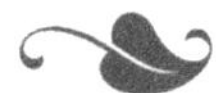

Arrival of the nuptial procession to the groom's village is one of the biggest shows of the marriage event. It is the time when the bride's relatives and friends exalt her. The procession is controlled by women who appear in their best attire carrying bags of maize (ngwasang), fingers of millet (sang) and bags of guinea-corn (sar), new sleeping mats (ghamse fiysi) and new specially designed bamboo stools (antah-jin). These are gifts for the bride (nko-se vijin) each of which must receive compensation from the groom and his family. Before leaving the village, the bride and two of her bride maids (wonjin) are richly adorned with cam wood from head to toe.

Bridal Attire

The bride's dress comprises 12 yards of dyed hand-woven (munchi) cloth (Wandzei-kilang-lang) which is wrapped around her waistline five to six times. The free end of the cloth hangs loosely in front of the girl from her navel to the knee or below. When a princess is getting married, the cloth is red, and the loose end is adorned with cowries. She wears a beaded necklace with several strings (nshwaga). These beads are special, they are blue and are held together in the front by a large blue bead with white lines at each end (Sibang) The daughter of a lord (kibai) wears a hat made with black feathers (kinsii) and holds a shiny horse tail (deng). She is richly adorned with bangles or bracelets made of elephant tusks.

The women in the procession sing merrily as they accompany the bride to her new home. The first thing the groom's family does as compensation for the gifts brought is giving a bag full of special gifts to the bridal procession. This bag is sent back to the compound head of the girl's family. For a princess and the daughter of a lord, the groom's family gives a castrated goat or a ram with 200 cowries in the olden days. A basket of corn-fufu or pounded cocoyams (Kinjo ke kiban or Kinjo ke viku-u) with a bowl of meat (lang nyam) are added to the goat or the ram. These things are taken to the Fon or to the lord. As the procession approaches the groom's compound, the bride is hidden in the crowd under umbrellas so nobody in that compound can see her. The merry crowd sings and dances towards the door of the main building in the compound (ngai) as directed until the bride disappears into the house. This hiding of the bride is aimed at heightening the curiosity of the groom's family to see the bride. They must give presents before they can be allowed to catch a glimpse of the bride. When the bridal procession settles down, the first course of entertainment is provided. After receiving the entertainment, the rest of the evening is spent dancing, drinking and making customary demands from the groom's family such as peanuts, roasted chicken to feed the bride or firewood to warm up the house in which the bride is lodged. Such demands aim at showing their host the value they have of their daughter, the bride. When the bridegroom and his relatives come to greet the bride, they bring money and other gifts. The bride receives these gifts and hands them over to a woman designated to receive them. This is the first and last time the bridegroom and relatives see the bride during that day.

General Entertainment on the Second Day (Ntar vijin)

General entertainment on the second day is very worrisome for the host family. The bride's family sets out to express dissatisfaction at everything served to them. The guests reject everything given to them causing panic in the groom's family. They run around fetching more food or wine to appease their guests. Mean time their guests make fun of them terming them misfits in the art of entertainment. The hosts continue to plead with them and to persuade them to accept the things they offer. The bride on the other hand becomes anxious fearing that her husband would disgrace her by not adequately entertaining her family. The groom tries his best to show case his capabilities and outdo himself by providing what his guests want and even more than they want. Later in the night when children and younger people are asleep, the elder sister of the bridegroom or an elderly lady of the groom's compound goes to main house of the compound (ngai) where the bride is lodged, gives the lady sitting closest to the bride some money (200 cowries) and humbly tells the lady she has come to beg for the bride (m'lon jin). The bride is graciously released to her and she takes her quickly to her brother's house. At four in the morning, the same lady goes to the groom's house taps the door and asked for the bride. The bride is released to her, she takes her back to the main house where she sleeps for a short time and is given a bath and cam wood is re-applied on her body.

Compensation for the Gifts brought by the Bridal Procession (Kani Nko)

While the guests are enjoying themselves, the hosts start to sort out the gifts brought by the bride's family assigning token compensation for each gift. In the olden days, compensation ranged from 200-500 cowries or 9 pennies to five shillings (when the British pound was the medium of exchange) according to the rank of donor in the bride's family. Each bag with gifts is given back to the owner with an amount of money as compensation for the gift. Many of these people can reject this compensation if they are not satisfied with the equity of the money to the gift they brought.

They indicate by throwing their bags back to the hosts, who then add some money and return them. When the women have at last accepted the compensation, they retire to prepare for the next stage. It is customary for them not to express complete satisfaction with the compensation.

The Bridal Show Dance (Fir jin)

The bridal show dance is the most exciting and enjoyable stage of in the Nso traditional marriage. It is the climax of the wedding celebrations. It is the exclusively reserved for the daughters of lords or princesses. It would be against the Nso tradition to stage the dance for a commoner's daughter. Christian women in Nso have defied this restriction and have staged the bridal show dance for all daughters. After general entertainment (ntar vijin), the bridal show dance begins. Music is organized by members of the wife's family who are experts at playing various musical instruments. As music plays, people of both the groom and bride's family dance in opposing lines facing each other dressed in their best. As the dance progresses, the bridegroom's relatives offer the gifts, first to the bride and then to the members of her family. Dancing alongside the bride is a maiden carrying a brand-new raffia bag in which she puts the monetary gifts. Two other women dancing near the bride receive the live chickens and hand them over to their friends as pre-arrange. The stepping forth of the bridegroom bearing a live chicken for the bride is greeted with shouts of excitement and more intense and additional melody to the music. The bride adds more style to her dancing and bends forward as she dances towards the groom. The groom dances confidently and with pride towards his bride. If both the bride and groom are good dancers, they take a long time to exchange their gifts. They dance gracefully towards each other retreat and then forward again several times tantalizing each other with the presents. They gently brush each other's face with the chickens to the admiration of the crowed which during the melodious music shouts excitedly acknowledging beauty of the occasion. After the exchange of gifts, the bride begins to give out her own gifts, first to the groom's relatives who have been introduced to her. Next, she gives gifts to her people and then turns to the musicians. She sticks coins on their forehead amidst loud applause. Lastly, the bride showers a large amount of coins to the crowd which goes scrambling for them. This impressive gesture ends the dance. The bride is taken to the grand hall (ngai vijin) where some of her relatives bid her farewell and depart for their village. The bride is left with a few girls from her village and bridesmaids who stay with her for another week and gradually hand her over to her husband's relatives. The length of stay of the bridesmaids depends on the hospitality of the groom's people.

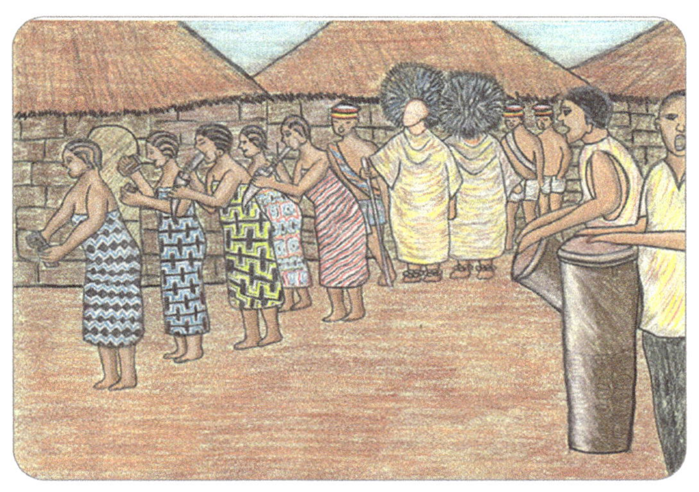

Musicians go to the gathering space to
prepare for the show dance

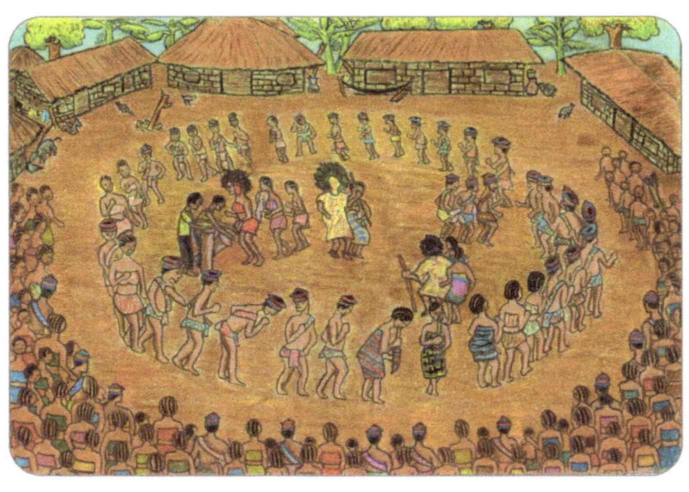

Festive dancers form a circle while an audience
watch and enjoy the whole scene.

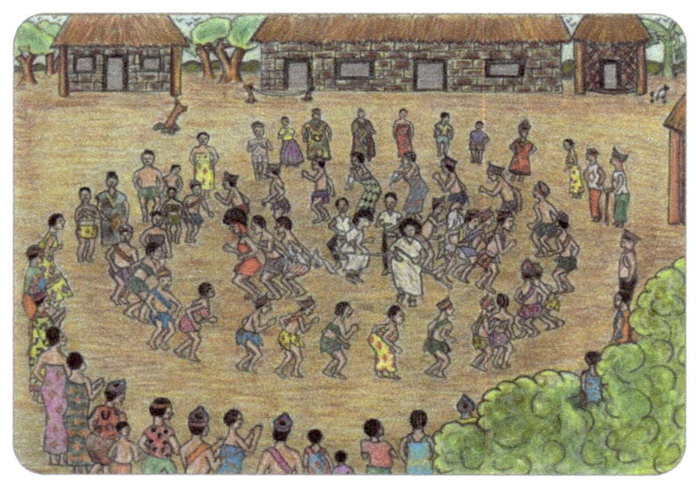

More festive dancing

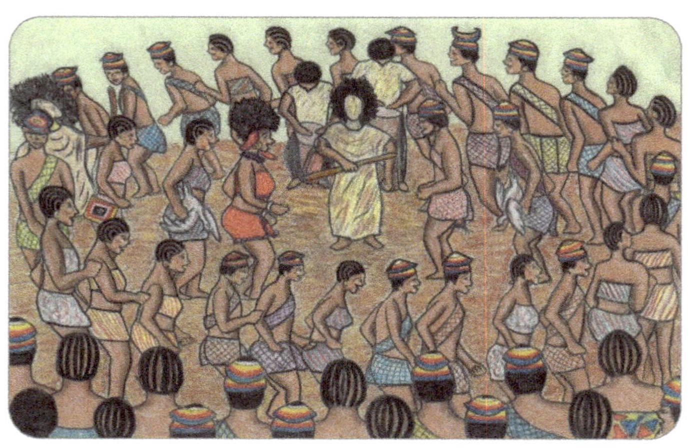

Bride and groom and their party dance facing each other

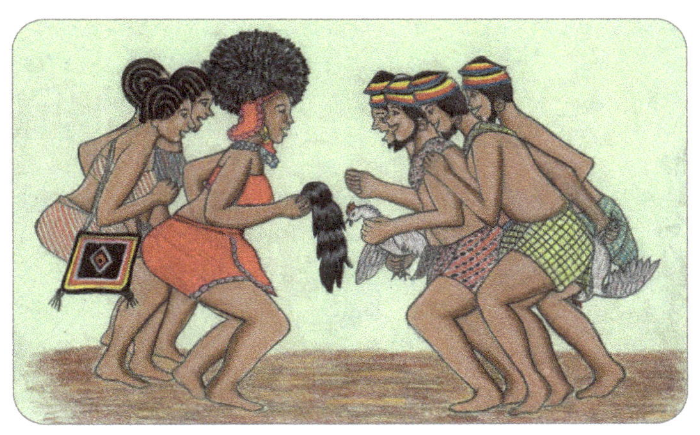

Dancing intensifies as bride, groom maids
and groom's men move to the center

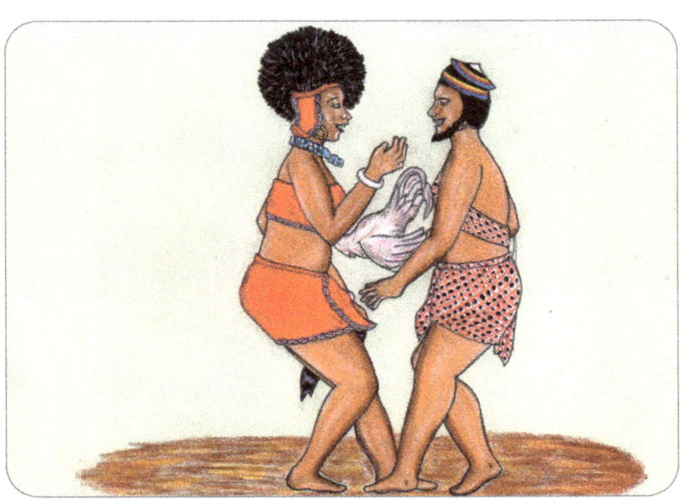

The men and maids step aside as the couple demonstrate
their dance styles triggering shouts of jubilation
(buh rir) from the crowd. Anybody in the crowd
can reward the couple with money or chicken

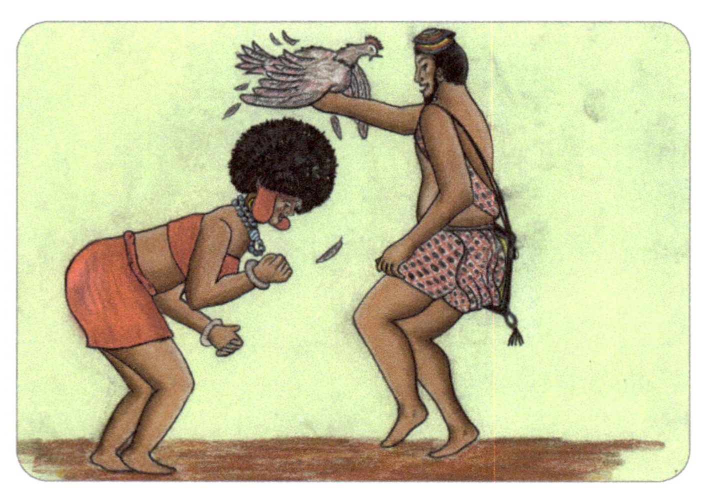

Groom rewards his bride. Crowd goes hysterical

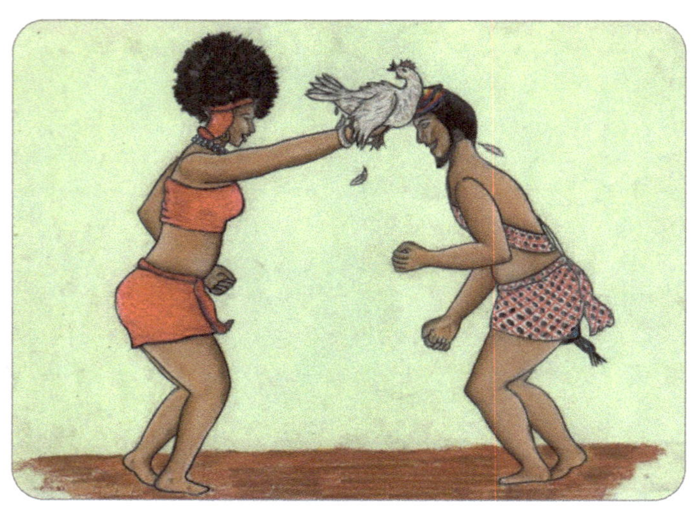

Sweeping of live chicken over her groom
draws shouts of jubilation

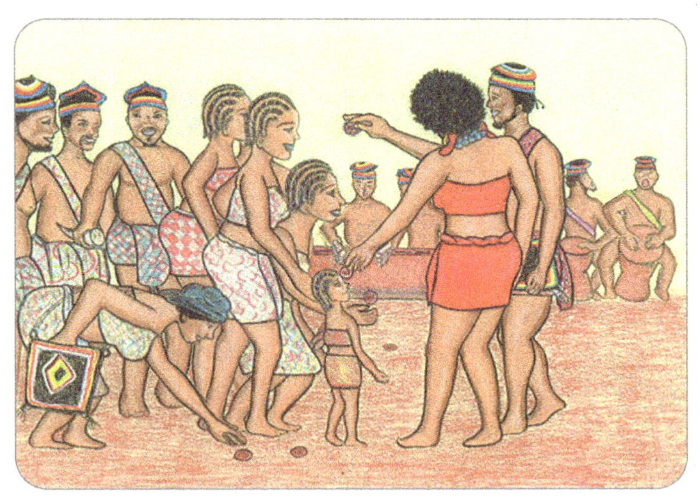

The bride and groom reward musicians, bride's
family, and any member of the publics

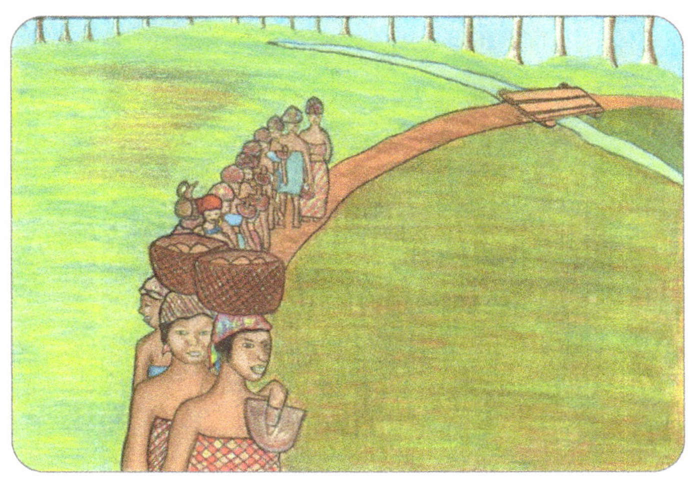

A group of women in the groom's compound
are taking the bride to her first farm

Taking of the Bride to her New Farm

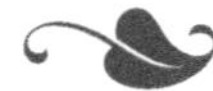

The taking of a newly married woman to a farm already reserved for her by her in- laws is an important event in the Nso tradition (fer jin kwa). All women in her new compound and friendly neighbors accompany her to the farm. Sometimes the bride's relatives turn up for this event. They all leave the compound in a single file placing the bride in the middle. They take along food and palm wine for their enjoyment. The women of this compound demonstrate their love for the bride by helping her till an extensive area of the farm. The bride is not allowed to till the farm on this day. She sits somewhere in a shaded area and periodically walks around to the women to express her gratitude for their assistance. She gives the women kolanuts as she walks around. This party of women does not stay in the farm till evening as is in normal circumstances. On their return home, the bride is given a bath. Sometimes a dance is staged in honor of this occasion which takes place two weeks after the wedding.

Pregnant Brides

In Nso, pregnancy before marriage is the greatest disgrace a girl can bring to the family. The girls' relatives are upset with her because she has deprived them of marriage gifts and particularly their pride. It also implies that the girl's family is incapable of bringing up girls with good moral fortitude for proper marriage. Pregnancy also deprives the girl of wedding festivities. The girl is taken to her husband secretly by two male relatives. After a week, five women are sent by her father to the girl's new compound to give her a bath. This delegation is often treated in a lukewarm manner by the girl's husband and relatives. The family of the girl does not blame her husband and his family for this lack of respect. This behavior is seen as a punishment for the girl's misbehavior.

Unorthodox Marriage (Kinchem)

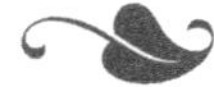

Taking a wife without formal proceedings in Nso custom is called kinchem or ncemi. Children born of such a marriage belong to the wife's parents. The husband is labeled a male goat (kibev) because he has no claim over his children. In some cases, this marriage receives recognition later when the father of the woman realizes that his daughter has a good home, blessed with many children, and is well cared for by her husband. At this point, the husband and his relatives can take gifts to the girl's family (juu). If there has been no previous grudge or problems between the family of the woman and that of the husband, the marriage is recognized. Grudges like seizure of property and adultery can cause the union never to be recognized. It is assumed that such a marriage never last long because the marriage is not protected by custom and the girl can return to their compound with her children whenever she wants, even for the flimsiest reasons. If one of the children becomes chronically ill and a soothsayer tells the girl that the form of marriage caused the illness and that all her children can die, the woman can decide to pack up and leave as fast as possible. Also, her husband may become seriously ill. This illness if attributed to the type of marriage, the woman can leave her husband immediately. It is also known that some fathers who have daughters in unorthodox marriage may want his in-laws to give all the marriage presents to him alone excluded the rest of his family members who are entitled to such gifts. This practice is condemned in the Nso tradition.

Marriage by Inheritance (villem)

Nso custom allows a man to inherit his son's, brother's, or father's widow. This practice ensures protection of women in a polygamous setting and explains why compound heads and traditional rulers have many wives and thus many children.

PART TWO

Methods of Wife Acquisition

How the Fon's sons acquired wives

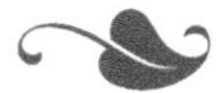

The Fon's sons (wonto) acquired wives in many ways. An active and outgoing young man who had been going to markets, attending festive occasions, going to large gatherings, participating in dancing, and drinking parties regularly with the hope of meeting beautiful girls is likely to find one he likes. This young man usually carried a pipe, a stick or a horse's tail (kisang) used for dancing and a cup used for drinking palm wine (bar melu). He usually gave either of these items to the girl he met and liked instructing her to take it to his house. If she did, she would be held there as his wife (kincem). If the young man had no article with which to woe the girl, he would point the girl out to his sisters asking them to get her for him. They would trick the girl arrest and forcibly take her to their brother who kept him as his wife. The young man then sent a message to the girl's parents to explain her absence from their home. The parents of the girl had no choice, but to accept this arrangement for fear of traditional reprisal and for respect of the Fon. The Fon then asked his son to bring gifts in the form of palm wine and kolanuts which were taken to the girl's parents as required marriage gifts (juu)

If the Fon's son (wanto) was lazy never attended any festivities, the Fon had to give him a wife. The Fon would ask any compound head of the Nshelaf or of the Duiy clan to give his son a wife. In this case he had to accept any girl given to him. Another way in which the Fon's sons acquired wives was by being friendly to a compound head that would reward his good behavior by giving him a wife. At times, a compound head (tarla) could decide to give his daughter in marriage to the Fon's son (wanto) to gain favors from the Fon. The mother of this girl had to come from the Nselaf or Duiy family. If the mother of the girl came from the M'ntar family, the compound head's right to give the girl's first daughter in marriage and receive gifts was forfeited. He did not also have any rights over her first-born son.

In the days of slavery, the Fon often gave male or female slaves as babysitters (a-liy-won) for the Fon's children (wonto). If a wanto got both a male and female babysitter, they could marry each other. When their female offspring became of age, she could be given to the Fon's son as a wife. If the wanto (Fon's son) was given a female slave as babysitter, she could be given in marriage to anybody, except to a wanto. The Fon's son could later chose to marry the daughter of the slave. In any of these cases, the wanto was not obligated take gifts to the slaves.

Ways by which a Fon Acquired his Wives

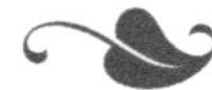

The Fon got his wives from prominent compound heads (atarla) of the Nselaf family. The Nso tradition mandated prominent atarla from the Nselaf family to give one of their daughters to the Fon as a wife (wiynto) and one of the sons to the palace who became one of the Fon's attendants (Nshiylaf). Compound heads (atarla) who did not hold high traditional status and wished to give their daughters in marriage to the palace could only give them to the Fon's sons.

If elderly Fon's wives are interested in any daughter of Nselaf family, they went to the house of the girl's father and apply calm wood (Bii) on the pillar at the center of the floor (kisengri). This was a sign that mandated the man to give one of his daughters to the Fon as a wife.

A compound head (tarla) of the M'ntar family who wished to give his daughter to the Fon could be given through a prominent compound head of the Nselaf clan. This tarla made efforts to get into the good graces of the Fon. By so doing, the son will accept his daughter as a wife. The son of this wife (wiynto) from the M'ntar family was usually made the Fon of Nso when the ruling Fon died (In lamsno the Fon does not die, he gets missing- Fon lai)

If a girl of the M'ntar family entered the Fon's farm to harvest any crop and was seen by a wiynto, she was arrested and taken to the palace to become a wiynto.

Ways of Giving the Fon's Daughters in Marriage

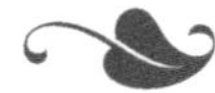

The Fon's daughters remained in the palace with their mothers until they were of marriageable age. Their mothers then went to Fai Mamo or to any tarnto (spokesperson for the Fon) and told him that her daughter was grown up. Fai Mamo as the head of the atarnto invited another tarnto preferably the one who was friendly to him and ask him to bring wine and firewood. Fai kept these items for himself. He informed the tarla that the Fon wanted to honor him with a wife (bu wun). The tarnto would tell the tarla the name of the girl's mother and investigations would begin to ensure that there were no hurdles. Obstacles to this process included close biological relationship of the tarla to the girl or an altercation with the girl's mother or her family. If every hurdle was cleared, the tarla was asked to bring firewood, a large calabash of wine and a big cock or rooster (kiyuv). The Tarnto and the Tarla took these items to the Fon who was informed about the name of his daughter (wanto) to be given in marriage. After this visit, the Fon's wives (vikiynto) determine the time and manner of handing the girl over to her future husband. This process has been discussed in the first part of this book.

How the Fon's Guards (Nshiyselaf) Got Wives

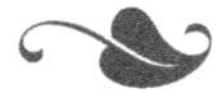

The Nshelaf clan in Nso is made up of two sub-groups; nshiyselav se Fai, those who wait on the Fon and nshiyselav se ngwerong are retainers of the ngwerong section of the palace. Of these two groups, nshiyselav se Fai were more favored in getting wives than nshiyselav se ngwerong. Normally an ordinary nshiylav could not marry a Fon's or Fai's daughter. The Duiy and the M'ntar families were reluctant to give their daughters in marriage to nshiyselav se ngwerong. They preferred to give their daughters to nshiyselav se Fai (atar dzee) so that if they had any problems to present to the Fon, their sons- in-law would influence their issue to their benefit. Most of the ordinary nshiyselav got married to the daughters of other nshiyselav. Some of the nshiyselav abducted daughters of the Dui and the M'ntar families from public events and marketplaces and married them. To prevent this behavior, the Duiy and M'ntar families restricted movements of their daughters. When a nshiylav died, the Fon gave the widow in marriage to another nshiylav. Female slaves and daughters of slaves were given in marriage to nshiyselav by the Fon. Men of the Duiy families got their wives from the M'ntar or Nshelaf families. M'ntar families married among themselves.

About Original Authors

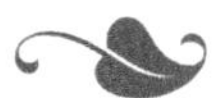

William Banboye

He served as representative of Catholic Education in Cameroon, catholic education secretary of Northwest and Southwest provinces of Cameroon, and National president of Nso Language organization. He was also the second principal of St. Augustine's secondary school Nso. Decorated with the Papal Medal of Honor, knighted with Cameroon medal of honor. He obtained a Bachelor of arts degree in History from Ottawa, Canada and earned a Diploma in French.

Fonka Shang Lawrence

My beloved father was former president of Cameroon National Assembly, member of parliament of Cameroon National Assembly, former junior minister of information in the Federal Republic of Nigeria, teacher and headmaster of St Teresa's school in Kimbo, Nso and later in his village of Sob, in Nso. He also served as part time teacher in St Augutine's secondary school in Nso. He was founding member of Nso credit union, president of Nso improvement union and member of the Nso history society. Coauthored Nso Marriage custom and Folk tales of Nso

Margaret Fonka Niba

I was born in Nso in the western part of Cameroon to parents Fonka Shang Lawrence and Odilia Fonka. I obtained my primary education in Shisong girls' school and in Saint Theresa's school Kimbo in Nso. I completed my secondary education in St. Augustine's college still in Nso. I did my professional nursing education in Bamenda Nursing School obtaining a practical nursing, diploma, and psychiatric nursing certificates. I enrolled in a nursing program in Delaware State University in Delaware, USA where I obtained Bachelor of Science in Nursing with a minor in Biology. Obtained my Master of Science in Nursing education in Grand Canyon University in Phoenix, Arizona USA. Presently retired from nursing.